R·S·V·P
Journal
Recovery • Spirituality • Vision • Purpose

Julie Rochelle, M.M.

Ambassador Press, LLC

in the spirit of excellence

Reynoldsburg, Ohio

Published by Ambassador Press, LLC
PO Box 722 Reynoldsburg, OH 43068
ambpress@insight.rr.com
www.ambassadorpressllc.com

Published in association with Julie Rochelle, M.M.
Visit us online at www.julierochelle.com

ISBN 10: 0-9787850-4-5
ISBN 13: 978-0-9787850-4-8

First Ambassador Press, LLC printing, October 2008

Dedication

I dedicate this book to my daughters: Maya, Mariah and Taylor. Thank you for your support, encouragement and spirit; your honesty, forgiveness and strength. You are my joy. I love being your mother most of all. Love is you.

And this journal is dedicated to all the brave and pioneering people who believe in recovery from addiction, are devoted to helping and being helped and to the families that love them. Bless those who are still suffering.

And to my mother, the strongest woman I have ever known. Your generosity and spirit inspire me each day.

Thanks to Megan Royle, Kristen Eckstein and Stacey Fisher for believing in this book project. To my clients, friends and family who have supported and encouraged me. A special thanks to Beth, Cher Bear, Amirra, Klazina, Johnnie and Diane who held my hand and walked me to the other side.

I will never forget your love and commitment.

-Julie Rochelle

About The Journal

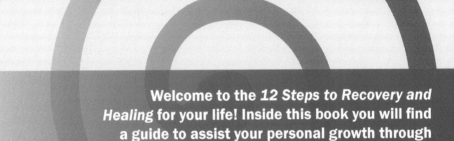

Welcome to the *12 Steps to Recovery and Healing* for your life! Inside this book you will find a guide to assist your personal growth through issues, addictions, change, loss and trauma.

This book will help you change patterns of behavior and thinking that created a slow degenerative decline in your mental, spiritual, emotional and physical health. As you recover and identify these blocks you will create healing in your life. There are solutions for your troubles. These are guidelines and suggestions.

This book is for you. It can also be used in a group, with your sponsor, counselor, minister or friends.

There are companion *RSVP Recovery Meditation Cards*: healing tools to help you focus your intent as you move forward toward personal growth. They can be purchased separately.

The 12 Steps

Step 1: We admitted we were powerless over _____; that our lives had become unmanageable.

Step 2: Came to believe that a power greater than ourselves could restore us to sanity.

Step 3: Made a decision to turn our will and our lives over to the care of God *as we understood Him.*

Step 4: Made a searching and fearless moral inventory of ourselves.

Step 5: Admitted to God, to ourselves and to another human being the exact nature of our wrongs.

Step 6: Were entirely ready to have God remove all these defects of character.

Step 7: Humbly asked Him to remove our shortcomings.

Step 8: Made a list of all persons we had harmed, and became willing to make amends to them all.

Step 9: Made direct amends to such people wherever possible, except when to do so would injure them or others.

Step 10: Continued to take personal inventory and when we were wrong promptly admitted it.

Step 11: Sought through prayer and meditation to improve our conscious contact with God *as we understood Him*, praying only for knowledge of His will for us and the power to carry that out.

Step 12: Having had a spiritual awakening as a result of these steps, we tried to carry this message to _____, and to practice these principles in all our affairs.

Serenity

God grant me the serenity to accept the things I cannot change, courage to change the things I can and the wisdom to know the difference.

Recovery

Imagine...Bringing your light to life—moving from darkness into the light. Discover who you are, find your voice, share your truth and value your life. Be whole once again. Your life is calling out to you for rest, reflection, recovery and renewal.

Enter the spiral—the sacred circle—and let the journey begin.

Love, Julie

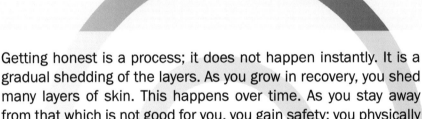

We admitted we were powerless over _____;
that our lives had become unmanageable.

Getting honest is a process; it does not happen instantly. It is a gradual shedding of the layers. As you grow in recovery, you shed many layers of skin. This happens over time. As you stay away from that which is not good for you, you gain safety; you physically heal. The fog begins to lift and you begin your journey towards *Honesty*. Keeping yourself safe is your job description. Protect yourself. Know your vulnerabilities. Addiction is cunning, baffling, powerful and patient.

Admitted

Recovery: Acts of Honesty

_____

_____

_____

_____

_____

_____

_____

_____

_____

_____

_____

_____

_____

_____

_____

_____

I accept me just as I am.

Recovery: Acts of Honesty

Recovery: Acts of Honesty

_____

_____

_____

_____

_____

_____

_____

_____

_____

_____

In *Step 1* we must find acceptance. We are sick and tired of being sick and tired. From the bottom we have no where to go but up. Once we stop fighting and admit that we can go no further, our journey will begin. We are humble now and need help. We used all our resources and now we know and admit our unmanageability. We will not get better on our own. We must hit bottom before we can change our thinking, attitudes, friends, beliefs and actions. Now we are teachable and ready to look truthfully into our own eyes and admit our need for help.

I know that powerlessness is my power today.

_____

_____

_____

_____

_____

_____

_____

_____

_____

_____

_____

_____

_____

_____

Recovery: Acts of Honesty

Recovery: Acts of Honesty

_____

_____

_____

_____

_____

_____

_____

_____

_____

_____

_____

_____

_____

_____

_____

_____

_____

I am alive.

I am a miracle.

_____

_____

_____

_____

_____

_____

_____

_____

_____

_____

_____

_____

_____

_____

_____

_____

_____

Recovery: Acts of Honesty

> *I will be amazed before I am half-way through.*

Dear God,

_____

_____

_____

_____

_____

_____

_____

_____

_____

_____

_____

_____

_____

_____

_____

_____

Recovery: Acts of Honesty

Step 2

Acts of Hope

Came to believe that a Power greater than ourselves could restore us to sanity.

Came, came to and came to believe! Thank goodness the program gives us all the time we need to find sanity. A power greater than ourselves is not defined for us. We define this for ourselves. We have plenty of time to figure it out. There is hope and we can open up to receive, open our minds and our hearts. If we walk five miles into the woods, we have to walk five miles out. This is a process, not an event. Keep walking down the road.

Believe

Recovery: Acts of Hope

I am thankful for sanity and sobriety.

_____

_____

_____

_____

_____

_____

_____

_____

_____

_____

_____

_____

_____

_____

_____

_____

_____

Recovery: Acts of Hope

Recovery: Acts of Hope

_____

_____

_____

_____

_____

_____

_____

_____

This whole "power greater than ourselves" business can be tricky. What do we know about trust? We have trouble trusting ourselves or others and now we are supposed to trust a power greater than ourselves?!? These are suggestions, not commandments. Keep an open mind, follow the suggestions and give yourself time and love. Take what works for you and leave the rest. This is a gentle and progressive growth. You have a whole lifetime to figure it out. Do not fight in your head, but listen to your heart. False pride can kill you, so pray for a humble heart. Stay out of ego and away from being self righteous. Defiance is problematic. Sometimes it saves lives; but now it is no longer a friend. Now it is time to believe: Thy will be done, not mine.

I am ready and know I am healing.

_____

_____

_____

_____

_____

_____

_____

_____

_____

_____

_____

_____

_____

_____

_____

_____

Recovery: Acts of Hope

Recovery: Acts of Hope

God grant me serenity
just for today.

Recovery: Acts of Hope

> *I am going to know a new freedom and a new happiness.*

Dear God,

_____

_____

_____

_____

_____

_____

_____

_____

_____

_____

_____

_____

_____

_____

_____

Step 3
Acts of Grace

Made a decision to turn our will and our lives over to the care of God as we understand Him.

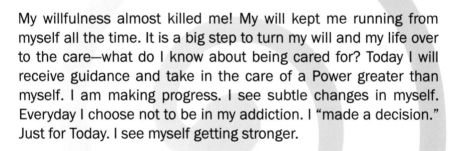

My willfulness almost killed me! My will kept me running from myself all the time. It is a big step to turn my will and my life over to the care—what do I know about being cared for? Today I will receive guidance and take in the care of a Power greater than myself. I am making progress. I see subtle changes in myself. Everyday I choose not to be in my addiction. I "made a decision." Just for Today. I see myself getting stronger.

Decision

Recovery: Acts of Grace

_____

_____

_____

_____

_____

_____

_____

_____

_____

_____

_____

_____

_____

_____

_____

_____

I am teachable.

_____
_____
_____
_____
_____
_____
_____
_____
_____
_____
_____
_____
_____
_____
_____
_____

Recovery: Acts of Grace

_____

_____

_____

_____

_____

_____

_____

_____

_____

_____

_____

We get to make a decision when we are ready. We are willing to open up. Self-will is a runaway train headed for a collision. This is our leap of faith: To let go of self-will and allow God's love and care to enter our heart and do some repair work. Once our self-will has been surrendered and we unload, we experience a new freedom. We regain trust and become less self-destructive. Now we get a new chance. We made a decision and each day is a new start.

Miracles happen. Look at me.

_____

_____

_____

_____

_____

_____

_____

_____

_____

_____

_____

_____

_____

_____

_____

Recovery: Acts of Grace

Recovery: Acts of Grace

_____

_____

_____

_____

_____

_____

_____

_____

_____

_____

_____

_____

_____

_____

_____

_____

Today my life is
perfect.

Recovery: Acts of Grace

> *I will not regret the past nor wish to shut the door on it.*

Dear God, _____

_____

_____

_____

_____

_____

_____

_____

_____

_____

_____

_____

_____

_____

Recovery: Acts of Grace

3rd Step Prayer

"God, I offer myself to thee - to build with me and to do with me as Thou wilt. Relieve me of the bondage of self, that I may better do Thy will. Take away my difficulties, that victory over them may bear witness to those I would help of Thy Power, Thy Love and Thy Way of life. May I do Thy will always."

Spirituality

Imagine... Bringing your light to life—moving from darkness into the light. Discover who you are, find your voice, share your truth and value your life. Be whole once again. Your life is calling out to you for rest, reflection, recovery and renewal.

Enter the spiral—the sacred circle—and let the journey begin.

Love, Julie

Acts of Courage

Made a searching and fearless moral
inventory of ourselves.

The shame can be so heavy. It takes great courage to dig down
deep and clear the clutter; clean our emotional house. It is brave
to be a human who is searching and growing, walking without
fear into the unknown. This step needs to be done in a thorough
manner and quickly. Dig in, do it and move forward to Step 5. Do
not get stuck here. We need support to get this done! Now I will
not blame, make excuses, justify or deny. I am learning discipline.
I know who I have been and who I am becoming. The truth will set
me free.

Inventory

Spirituality: Acts of Courage

_____

_____

_____

_____

_____

_____

_____

_____

_____

_____

_____

_____

_____

_____

_____

_____

I am honest today.

_____

_____

_____

_____

_____

_____

_____

_____

_____

_____

_____

_____

_____

_____

_____

Spirituality: Acts of Courage

_____

_____

_____

_____

_____

_____

_____

_____

_____

I look at myself honestly and I am piecing together my story. I admit my wrongs. I am discovering what my strengths are and I am writing about my unfinished business—the heavy baggage I am carrying. Now I am discovering why I struggle with low self-esteem. My past actions and resentments are being written down as I move through _Step 4_. I will be honest. My self-awareness is growing. In _Step 4_ I begin to realize how I got my low self-esteem and how irresponsible I became with my life and emotions. I blocked my feelings. My feelings are the path to the soul, so I blocked my soul self. Chaos took over. Resentments, fears, anger and denial—I wrote all these down.

Be specific. Tell your story to yourself. Explore your beliefs, behaviors and attitudes so you can have a bright future.

I am free from the baggage of the past;
I live for today.

_____

_____

_____

_____

_____

_____

_____

_____

_____

_____

_____

_____

_____

_____

Spirituality: Acts of Courage

Spirituality: Acts of Courage

_____

_____

_____

_____

_____

_____

_____

_____

_____

_____

_____

_____

_____

_____

I am safe.

_____

_____

_____

_____

_____

_____

_____

_____

_____

_____

_____

_____

_____

_____

_____

_____

Spirituality: Acts of Courage

> *I will comprehend the word serenity*
> *and I will know peace.*

Spirituality: Acts of Courage

Dear God,

_____

_____

_____

_____

_____

_____

_____

_____

_____

_____

_____

_____

_____

_____

Step 5

Acts of Integrity

Admitted to God, to ourselves and to another human being the exact nature of our wrongs.

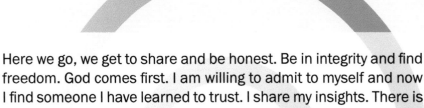

Here we go, we get to share and be honest. Be in integrity and find freedom. God comes first. I am willing to admit to myself and now I find someone I have learned to trust. I share my insights. There is help for me with help from my Higher Power. I know who I am and I know I cannot do this alone. It is a great relief to speak the truth and have someone respectfully listen without judgment and to be heard and understood.

Admitted

Spirituality: Acts of Integrity

_____

_____

_____

_____

_____

_____

_____

_____

_____

_____

_____

_____

_____

_____

_____

> *I am a bell that rings true.*
> *My "Outerds" match my "Innerds."*

_____

_____

_____

_____

_____

_____

_____

_____

_____

_____

_____

_____

_____

_____

_____

_____

Spirituality: Acts of Integrity

Spirituality: Acts of Integrity

_____

_____

_____

_____

_____

_____

_____

_____

_____

In _Step 5_ I will tell my story and I will be totally honest and admit my wrongs and shortcomings. I know this will help me learn more about honesty and trust. My Higher Power has helped me get this far and I am grateful. My heart is open as I tell the truth. I am safe to speak my truth; to never hide again! I will not isolate as I have in the past. I will let go, let God. I have looked in the mirror and now I honestly see who is looking back at me. I am honest and my heaviness is lifting.

I am responsible today for my thoughts, actions and words.

_____

_____

_____

_____

_____

_____

_____

_____

_____

_____

_____

_____

_____

_____

Spirituality: Acts of Integrity

Spirituality: Acts of Integrity

_____

_____

_____

_____

_____

_____

_____

_____

_____

_____

_____

_____

_____

_____

I am so relieved to be free.

Spirituality: Acts of Integrity

> *I will see how my experiences can benefit others.*

Dear God, _____

_____

_____

_____

_____

_____

_____

_____

_____

_____

_____

_____

_____

_____

Spirituality: Acts of Integrity

Step 6
Acts of Willingness

Were entirely ready to have God remove
all these defects of character.

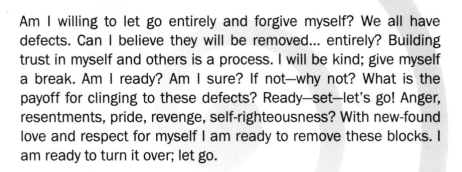

Am I willing to let go entirely and forgive myself? We all have
defects. Can I believe they will be removed... entirely? Building
trust in myself and others is a process. I will be kind; give myself
a break. Am I ready? Am I sure? If not—why not? What is the
payoff for clinging to these defects? Ready—set—let's go! Anger,
resentments, pride, revenge, self-righteousness? With new-found
love and respect for myself I am ready to remove these blocks. I
am ready to turn it over; let go.

Remove

Spirituality: Acts of Willingness

_____

_____

_____

_____

_____

_____

_____

_____

_____

_____

_____

_____

_____

_____

_____

I am strong, peaceful and growing.

_____

_____

_____

_____

_____

_____

_____

_____

_____

_____

_____

_____

_____

_____

Spirituality: Acts of Willingness

_____

_____

_____

_____

_____

_____

_____

_____

_____

In *Step 6* I am relieved and now realize that I am letting go of part of my identity, and a way of life. I am absorbing the changes I have made, giving myself time to make deep and subtle changes and asking for my Higher Power's help. I need time for reflection to soak it all in, find balance and center myself. "Were entirely ready" means I am making a big shift in behavior and consciousness. Getting ready to go on a trip is different from getting on the plane. I want change and I can see change in myself. I am willing, ready and able to change.

What is a defect? Examples are: blame, pride, envy, jealousy, self-righteousness, etc. Things that erode your character over time.

I am trustworthy.

I am learning to trust me.

_____

_____

_____

_____

_____

_____

_____

_____

_____

_____

_____

_____

_____

_____

_____

Spirituality: Acts of Willingness

Spirituality: Acts of Willingness

_____

_____

_____

_____

_____

_____

_____

_____

_____

_____

_____

_____

_____

_____

_____

> *I accept people and myself.*
> *Everything is as it should be*

_____

_____

_____

_____

_____

_____

_____

_____

_____

_____

_____

_____

_____

_____

_____

Spirituality: Acts of Willingness

That feeling of uselessness and
self-pity will disappear.

Dear God,

Vision

Imagine... Trusting yourself once again. Listen for your insight, hope, vitality, and meaning. Carry on in compassion, creation, health, and celebrate your progress.

Be inspired! Find the voice of your heart.

Enter the spiral—the sacred circle—and let the journey begin.

Love, Julie

Acts of

Humbly asked Him to remove our short comings.

To humbly ask without humiliation is new for us. Often we have lost our dignity in the past. Now we become teachable. Now we ask earnestly for deliverance from what has kept us bound up. Take this away.

It is hard to learn how to ask. I do not know everything and my best thinking got me to where I am today. I need help. I recognize my blocks and I am ready to change. "Help" is my simple prayer.

Remove

Simplicity keeps me manageable

_____

_____

_____

_____

_____

_____

_____

_____

_____

_____

_____

_____

_____

_____

_____

_____

_____

_____

_____

_____

_____

_____

Today I will pray with the humility of someone who has truly suffered. I know I have character defects and I turn it over each day. This Step is personal. This is a time to have my prayer become an intimate exchange between my Higher Power and my personal thoughts, words, feelings and truth. I open my heart and pray for guidance, hope, compassion and peace. Letting go of control, knowing who I truly am, I ask for guidance and for help in a good and humble way. Please remove the defects that create pain in our lives.

Now I can look forward. Healing takes time and focus. I get stronger by going to meetings, prayer, calling other people, working the steps and if necessary finding a counselor, minister or other professional. I am willing to go to any lengths! I see myself clearly and that makes me humble.

_____

_____

_____

_____

_____

_____

_____

_____

_____

_____

_____

_____

_____

_____

_____

_____

Open my heart, mind and soul.

*I will lose interest in selfish things and
I will gain interest in my fellows.*

Dear God, _____

_____

_____

_____

_____

_____

_____

_____

_____

_____

_____

_____

_____

_____

_____

Vision: *Acts of Humility*

7th Step Prayer

"My Creator, I am now willing that you should have all of me, good and bad. I pray that you now remove from me every single defect of character which stands in the way of my usefulness to you and my fellows. Grant me strength, as I go out from here, to do your bidding. Amen."

Acts of

Made a list of all persons we had harmed and became willing to make amends to them all.

Addictions hurt those who love us. It is a positive experience to make a list of persons we have harmed. We are being responsible for our actions, words and deeds. This step is a "getting ready" step. Get willing. It is not appropriate to rush out and make it right. It is appropriate to make a list and stop. There are people on your list that you will make amends to and there are people on your list you will not make amends to. As you work on this list the idea of making amends grows as you do.

Today you are responsible. You know who you are and what you need to do. Just do the next right thing.

Amends

I forgive myself and I forgive ot...

_____

_____

_____

_____

_____

_____

_____

_____

_____

_____

_____

_____

_____

_____

_____

_____

_____

_____

_____

_____

_____

_____

_____

_____

In *Steps 1–7* we have been focused on ourselves. Now we are ready to look beyond to see how our behavior has affected friends, family, creditors, etc. Now I am ready to take responsibility for my actions, words and addiction. I am willing, with help, to stop the blame game, forgive myself and realize that I have character defects that have harmed others. I will work through my resistance, guilt, shame and low self-esteem. I will accept the consequences and make restitution. I forgive myself and make it right.

My mind is open. My heart is open.

_____

_____

_____

_____

_____

_____

_____

_____

_____

_____

_____

_____

_____

_____

_____

I expect life to

awesome.

_____

_____

_____

_____

_____

_____

_____

_____

_____

_____

_____

_____

_____

_____

_____

_____

*f-seeking will
slip away.*

Dear God,

_____

_____

_____

_____

_____

_____

_____

_____

_____

_____

_____

_____

_____

_____

_____

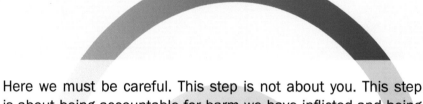

Acts of O...

Made direct amends to such people whenever possible except when to do so would injure them or others.

Here we must be careful. This step is not about you. This step is about being accountable for harm we have inflicted and being truly sorry. Opportunities will arise when we ask for God's help. Now I am ready so the situation will happen as it needs to. When you are ready, you will know what to say, what to do and what help you need. Stay in touch with your sponsor or a friend who can help you discern your timing. Pray for courage now. Suit up and show up.

Amends

I am a strong and
powerful woman/m

_____

_____

_____

_____

_____

_____

_____

_____

_____

_____

_____

_____

_____

Now we have a plan and it is time to go for it. We use the list we have made. Remember, we do no harm to others and none to ourselves. We talk in an honest way as we seek restitution or forgiveness.

I am released from the guilt and shame that used to keep me from freedom. I have courage and I will accept whatever consequences come to me as a result of my actions. I will keep my amends simple and to the point. I will pray hard, be sincere and let God do the work.

I choose peace and serenity

_____

_____

_____

_____

_____

_____

_____

_____

_____

_____

_____

_____

_____

_____

I talk, trust and feel today.

_____

_____

_____

_____

_____

_____

_____

_____

_____

_____

_____

_____

_____

_____

_____

_____

> *My whole attitude and outlook on life will change.*

Dear God,

_____

_____

_____

_____

_____

_____

_____

_____

_____

_____

_____

_____

_____

Purpose

Imagine... "I don't know what your destiny will be, but one thing I do know... the only ones among you who will be really happy are those who have sought and found how to serve."

-Albert Schweitzer

Enter the spiral—the sacred circle—and let the journey begin.

Love, Julie

Step 10

Acts of Perseverance

Continued to take personal inventory and when we were wrong promptly admitted it.

We are always growing in the program, being self-reflective, changing our lives as we continue on this path of serenity.

I clean up my messes quickly. I keep my house in order; I do this on a daily basis. I take care of myself in my life. Attitude check daily! I know now that recovery is a way of life. I will do this all my life. This is a good life. I am present and accountable.

Promptly

Purpose: Acts of Perseverance

I keep no secrets today.

_____

_____

_____

_____

_____

_____

_____

_____

_____

_____

_____

_____

_____

_____

Purpose: *Acts of Perseverance*

Purpose: *Acts of Perseverance*

_____

_____

_____

_____

_____

_____

_____

_____

_____

_____

Continuing to take "personal inventory" means we are constantly self-reflective. Making a personal inventory becomes a daily process. We don't let things pile up. Daily maintenance helps us have gratitude for all we have accomplished. We change and learn to love ourselves each day. We have the tools we need to repair any damage. We need to use these tools each day.

I write in my journal and I keep a regular inventory. I live in today, one day at a time.

I love who I am and what I do.

_____
_____
_____
_____
_____
_____
_____
_____
_____
_____
_____
_____
_____
_____
_____
_____

Purpose: Acts of Perseverance

Purpose: *Acts of Perseverance*

_____

_____

_____

_____

_____

_____

_____

_____

_____

_____

_____

_____

_____

_____

_____

My heart is expanding and so is my light.

_____

_____

_____

_____

_____

_____

_____

_____

_____

_____

_____

_____

_____

_____

_____

_____

Purpose: *Acts of Perseverance*

Fear of economic insecurity will leave me.

Dear God, _____

_____

_____

_____

_____

_____

_____

_____

_____

_____

_____

_____

_____

_____

_____

Step 11

Acts of Spirituality

Sought through prayer and meditation to improve our conscious contact with God, as we understood Him, praying only for knowledge of His will for us and the power to carry that out.

Each morning I am grateful for my sobriety. I meditate and pray, ask for guidance and help and give thanks for another day! I am growing spiritually. The God of my understanding is Love. This is a personal relationship I have with my Higher Power. I give this relationship a lot of time and energy because it deepens my spiritual contact. I do this often. I am a seeker. Thy will be done.

Improve

Purpose: *Acts of Spirituality*

Light and love flow through me.

_____

_____

_____

_____

_____

_____

_____

_____

_____

_____

_____

_____

_____

_____

_____

Purpose: Acts of Spirituality

Purpose: *Acts of Spirituality*

_____

_____

_____

_____

_____

_____

_____

_____

_____

_____

Today I live closer to my Higher Power. In prayer and meditation I receive guidance, support, honesty and healing. When I pray I am talking to my Higher Power. When I meditate, I am listening. Either way, I desire to have communication and know God's will for me. I am a seeker. I know I am guided and if I ask, I will find guidance, trust, self-esteem and gratitude. I give thanks because once I was lost, now I am healing. I feel comforted and peaceful. I turn it over, receive, give thanks and love.

> *I am grateful for my life.*
> *My heart is full.*

_____

_____

_____

_____

_____

_____

_____

_____

_____

_____

_____

_____

_____

_____

_____

Purpose: Acts of Spirituality

Purpose: *Acts of Spirituality*

Change and transformation are a normal part of my life.

_____

_____

_____

_____

_____

_____

_____

_____

_____

_____

_____

_____

_____

_____

_____

Purpose: *Acts of Spirituality*

I will intuitively know how to handle situations which used to baffle me.

Dear God,

_____
_____
_____
_____
_____
_____
_____
_____
_____
_____
_____
_____
_____
_____

Purpose: *Acts of Spirituality*

Step 12

Acts of Service

Having had a Spiritual Awakening as a result of these steps, we tried to carry this message to _____ and to practice these principles in all our affairs.

Today I know that I have a message to share with those who are still suffering. I practice these principles. I live a good life and live the serenity prayer as a part of my daily life. I live the steps by example. Walk the talk, do the footwork. I know I am a miracle. I expect miracles and I believe.

"Don't give up five minutes before the miracle happens." It is your destiny to be whole, happy and healed.

Awakening

Purpose: Acts of Service

_____

_____

_____

_____

_____

_____

_____

_____

_____

_____

_____

_____

_____

_____

_____

_____

_____

Service is my life.
I am grateful to be of service.
I am light.

_____

_____

_____

_____

_____

_____

_____

_____

_____

_____

_____

_____

_____

_____

Purpose: *Acts of Service*

Purpose: Acts of Service

_____

_____

_____

_____

_____

_____

_____

_____

_____

_____

I have had a spiritual awakening. I am on a spiritual journey. Recovery is a way of life. I see how far I have come. I am alive and growing. I am committed to change. I am growing and sharing my life. I have experience, strength and hope. I help others. I have something to share with others! I trust and say "Your will be done, not mine". These principles guide my life each day. I let go and live my life with honesty and courage. My life has been transformed and I see how far I have come. I will give back what has been given to me. I am committed to this recovery life. I know my recovery, spirituality and I have vision and purpose. RSVP. Keep Coming Back!

> *I nourish and care for myself and my sobriety.*

_____

_____

_____

_____

_____

_____

_____

_____

_____

_____

_____

_____

_____

_____

Purpose: *Acts of Service*

Purpose: Acts of Service

I take action today. I do the foot work.

_____

_____

_____

_____

_____

_____

_____

_____

_____

_____

_____

_____

_____

_____

_____

Purpose: Acts of Service

I will suddenly realize that God (of my understanding) is doing for me what I could not do for myself.

Dear God,

_____

_____

_____

_____

_____

_____

_____

_____

_____

_____

_____

_____

_____

_____

Purpose: Acts of Service

About Julie

Julie recognizes the global impact of healing and recovery throughout the world and is excited to offer this book in support for all those who are still suffering. Her 27 years of personal and professional development work include being an adjunct faculty member of Seattle University's School of Theology and Ministry. She is passionate about lifelong spirituality in recovery, leadership and organizational development and has taught conflict resolution and communications for over twenty years.

As a distinguished transformational life coach, Julie offers mentoring and motivation for addictions professionals and their clients. Recovery is her commitment. She is a mother, teacher and wise woman; a nationally-loved trainer, retreat director and consultant who inspires and facilitates deep change, inner focus and self-expression. It is with great integrity, humor and dedication that she speaks and teaches about acts of courage, power and love in the field of recovery.

RSVP Cards

Companion to the *RSVP Journal*

The *RSVP Meditation Recovery Cards for Healing* are tools that allow you to see deeper into the thoughts reflected in the journal as they relate to your life in the present moment. The cards give you insight into the direction of your life. These words are given to help you develop yourself, grow deeper spiritually and find meaning and purpose for your life in recovery.

Your intuition will guide you and help you find balance and clarity. The cards help you "pick a topic" for a meeting or for your life, one day at a time.

These cards may be purchased at www.julierochelle.com or by calling 336.887.0589

Printed in the United States
126865LV00001B